FOCUS ON CURRENT EVENTS

THE CLIMATE CRISIS

by Cynthia Kennedy Henzel

FOCUS
READERS®

VOYAGER

www.focusreaders.com

Focus Readers is distributed by North Star Editions:
sales@northstareditions.com | 888-417-0195

Produced for Focus Readers by Red Line Editorial.

Content Consultant: Dr. Andrea Drewes, Assistant Professor of Education and Human Services at Rider University

Photographs ©: Shutterstock Images, cover, 1, 9, 10–11, 13, 16–17, 21, 23, 24–25, 27, 34–35, 37, 45; Mohammed Seeneen/AP Images, 4–5; Advanced Spaceborne Thermal Emission and Reflection Radiometer (ASTER)/NASA, 7; Red Line Editorial, 15, 32; Kyle Miller/Wyoming Hotshots/USFS, 19; Steve Hillebrand/USFWS, 29; Abdeljalil Bounhar/AP Images, 30–31; Adam Fondren/Rapid City Journal/AP Images, 39; Luiz Rampelotto/EuropaNewswire/picture-alliance/dpa/AP Images, 41; Andrew Bossi/NASA, 42–43

Library of Congress Cataloging-in-Publication Data
Library of Congress Cataloging-in-Publication Data is available on the Library of Congress website.

ISBN
978-1-63739-075-7 (hardcover)
978-1-63739-129-7 (paperback)
978-1-63739-230-0 (ebook pdf)
978-1-63739-183-9 (hosted ebook)

Printed in the United States of America
Mankato, MN
012022

ABOUT THE AUTHOR

Cynthia Kennedy Henzel has a BS in social studies education and an MS in geography. She worked as a teacher-educator in many countries. Currently, she writes books and develops education materials for social studies, history, science, and ELL students. She has written more than 100 books for young people.

TABLE OF CONTENTS

17 OCTOBER 2009
REEFFISH
MALDIVES

Dr. Ibrahim Didi
Minister of Fisheries and Agriculture

CHAPTER 1

A GOVERNMENT UNDERWATER

President Mohamed Nasheed of Maldives sat underwater at a table on the ocean floor. He and members of his cabinet saw the surface of the water above them. Bubbles from their scuba equipment rose up. Curious fish swam by. Their country wasn't underwater—yet. But the leader of the island-nation was worried about **climate change**. He wanted the world's nations to agree to work together at a 2009 United Nations (UN)

In October 2009, government officials of Maldives held an underwater meeting to draw attention to climate change.

conference on climate. Unless leaders took action, the islands of Maldives could be drowned by the rising sea level. Nasheed's underwater cabinet meeting was a way to get the world's attention.

The Republic of Maldives is a country of approximately 1,200 islands. It is located south of India. The tropical country is home to more than half a million people. Maldives is also a vacation spot for more than 1.5 million tourists each year. Some come to relax in resorts. Some come to see the beautiful aqua-colored water and white beaches. Others come to scuba dive or snorkel.

Approximately 80 percent of Maldives is less than 3.3 feet (1.0 m) above sea level. The highest point in the entire country is no more than 8 feet (2.4 m) above sea level. As evidence showed that Earth's climate was warming, Maldivians worried. Higher temperatures had started melting glaciers

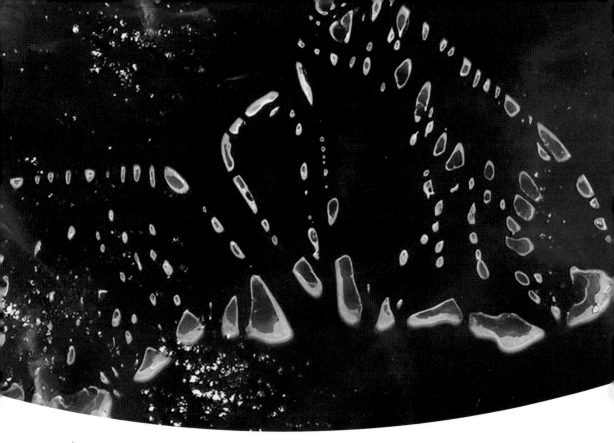

▲ The islands of Maldives are formed by rings of coral reefs. The coral reefs support thousands of species.

and ice sheets at the planet's poles. The melted ice was flowing into the ocean, causing the sea level to rise. Warm water also expands. This added to the rise in sea level.

Maldivians started preparing for the coming crisis. They built seawalls to hold back rising water. They created new islands that were at higher elevations. Workers scooped sand from the seafloor. Then they filled coral rings with the sand. These higher islands could provide a place to live if lower islands disappeared below the ocean. Still, violent storms have topped many of the seawalls. As a result, the government also looked into buying land from other countries. At some point, Maldivians may need to leave. By the 2020s, many people feared they would have to leave sooner rather than later.

The UN held a Climate Ambition Summit in 2020. Maldives's new president, Ibrahim Mohamed Solih, announced that Maldives could achieve net-zero emissions by 2030. Net-zero emissions means reaching a balance between produced emissions and removed emissions. Then Maldives would no longer contribute to global warming.

▲ Malé is the capital of Maldives. The city is surrounded by seawalls, which limited damage from a 2004 tsunami.

However, Maldives produces only 0.0003 percent of the air pollution, such as carbon dioxide (CO_2), that leads to climate change. So, Maldives worked to convince large industrial nations such as the United States and China to cut back. In 2020, those countries were not taking enough action. If nothing changed, the islands of Maldives could disappear by the end of the century.

CHAPTER 2

CAUSES OF CLIMATE CHANGE

Human-caused climate change began in the 1800s. The **Industrial Revolution** was the main reason why. Factories produced many goods. People started traveling by trains and steamships. These new technologies needed iron and steel. They also needed a lot of power to keep machines running. Fossil fuels provided most of that power.

In the 1890s, a scientist learned how fossil fuels affected the climate. When fossil fuels are

Coal is a rock formed from long-dead plants. Miners remove coal from the earth so it can be used for fuel.

burned, they release carbon dioxide. The ocean absorbs much of this gas. Plants also take in CO_2 during **photosynthesis**. But the rest enters the atmosphere. CO_2 in the atmosphere traps heat from the sun. Over time, higher levels of CO_2 lead to more trapped heat. And more trapped heat increases Earth's average temperature. This idea became known as the greenhouse effect.

At first, people mainly burned coal for fuel. In the early 1900s, people began using lots of oil as well. They often turned the oil into gasoline. That powered vehicles such as cars. In the mid-1900s, natural gas became a third major fossil fuel source. Natural gas often produced electricity and heat for homes and buildings. These three fossil fuels put massive amounts of CO_2 into the air.

Using fossil fuels for machines is the main way people produce excess CO_2. But it's not the only

In 2021, more than 40 percent of the oil drilled in the United States came from Texas.

way. People also cut down huge areas of forests for cities and farms. Clearing forests releases CO_2 back into the air. It also means there are fewer plants to take CO_2 out of the atmosphere.

CO_2 makes up approximately two-thirds of all global greenhouse gas emissions. But people produce other greenhouse gases, too. For instance, using excess fertilizer leads to more nitrous oxide. The other major greenhouse gas is methane. Methane is released in several ways. One way is by waste in landfills. Another is in agriculture, especially in growing rice. These and other greenhouse gases also trap heat in the air.

In the 1950s, scientists looked again at the greenhouse effect. They found evidence that increases in CO_2 did warm the atmosphere. In 1960, another scientist proved that the level of CO_2 in Earth's atmosphere was rising each year. By the 1980s, scientists widely agreed that humans were causing climate change.

Even so, fossil fuel use continued to soar. As a result, Earth had warmed more than 2 degrees Fahrenheit (1°C) since before the Industrial Revolution. The United States was the nation most responsible. Between the 1750s and 2010s, the United States produced approximately 25 percent of all CO_2 emissions. Other nations played large roles, too. For example, China became the largest fossil-fuel user in the 2000s. In contrast, South American and African countries produced just 6 percent of total emissions.

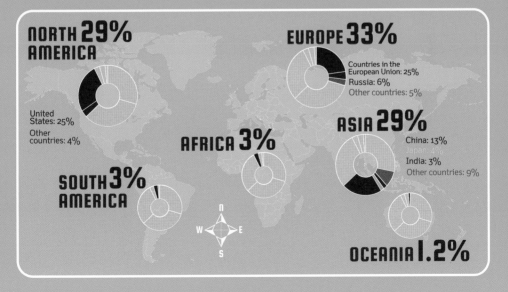

CO_2 EMISSIONS BY REGION ◄

This map shows how much countries and continents have contributed to global CO_2 emissions between 1751 and 2017.

NORTH AMERICA 29%

United States: 25%
Other countries: 4%

SOUTH AMERICA 3%

AFRICA 3%

EUROPE 33%

Countries in the European Union: 25%
Russia: 6%
Other countries: 5%

ASIA 29%

China: 13%
Japan: 4%
India: 3%
Other countries: 9%

OCEANIA 1.2%

N
W E
S

CHAPTER 3

EFFECTS OF CLIMATE CHANGE

The climate crisis is causing many changes. Earth's average temperature is rising. As a result, sea levels are rising, too. Sea level rise most directly affects coastal areas. It increases flooding and shore erosion, and it makes storms more dangerous. It has forced many people to move. As sea levels keep rising, more people will be affected. By 2100, hundreds of millions of people in low coastal areas might have to move.

Between 1880 and 2020, the global sea level rose approximately 8 to 9 inches (20–23 cm). By 2100, the sea level could rise as much as 8 feet (2.4 m).

The climate crisis is also changing weather patterns. As a result, some places are having more droughts and heat waves. Wildfires are growing in size and intensity. Meanwhile, other places are experiencing more rain and flooding.

A warmer planet means there is more energy in the atmosphere. Warm air holds more water than cool air. This can cause stronger storms with more rain and winds. Hurricanes, which begin in the tropics, need sea surface temperatures greater than 79 degrees Fahrenheit (26°C) to form and grow. So, warming seas mean more frequent hurricanes. From 1995 to 2020, there were 17 above-normal Atlantic hurricane seasons.

The habitats of animals and plants are changing, too. Wildfires are destroying more forests. Huge numbers of animals can die in these fires. Animals that survive often have to move to

In August 2020, the Pine Gulch Fire became the largest wildfire in Colorado history.

find food and shelter. Sea life is also impacted. Many animals cannot survive in water at high temperatures. But heat isn't the only problem. Oceans are absorbing more and more carbon dioxide. This is making the water more **acidic**. Coral and other sea life often die as a result.

Changing ecosystems affect people as well. For example, many agricultural areas are turning into deserts. These areas are too dry to grow crops or feed livestock. In many cases, people must migrate to new areas. People who migrate often undertake dangerous journeys. And the places they go often don't welcome them. These changes can lead to many kinds of conflict.

Climate change is already happening, and its impacts can be felt everywhere on Earth. However, the crisis is affecting some people much more than others. Tropical areas and island-nations have been especially impacted. Extreme tropical storms have hit countries such as Haiti, Japan, and the Philippines. India, Kenya, and Rwanda were home to floods that destroyed thousands of homes.

➤ THINK ABOUT IT

How is climate change affecting where you live?

Two hurricanes hit Nicaragua, Honduras, and Guatemala in November 2020. Many people struggled to recover.

Wealth plays a major role in how strongly climate change affects people. Wealthy countries and people are more able to recover than low-income countries and people are. Wealthy nations and people can pay to adapt to extreme weather. They have more money to help move or rebuild. Low-income countries and people do not. People can lose everything when floods, storms, or droughts destroy their land.

SPREADING DISEASE

Climate change is increasing the risk of disease spread. One reason is that most new **pathogens** come from animals. For example, many kinds of mosquitoes carry pathogens. Mosquitoes require warm areas to survive. So, they die in cold winters. However, as winters warm, mosquitoes spread to new regions. Some bring pathogens along with them. Then people can get diseases they've never been exposed to before.

Another reason is that climate change is reducing **biodiversity**. Less-diverse ecosystems allow for greater spread of disease. For instance, deer ticks carry bacteria that lead to Lyme disease. These ticks can give the bacteria to mice and opossums. The mice often spread the bacteria back to other ticks. Opossums kill most ticks that feed on them. So, they don't spread the bacteria as much. As a result, areas with both

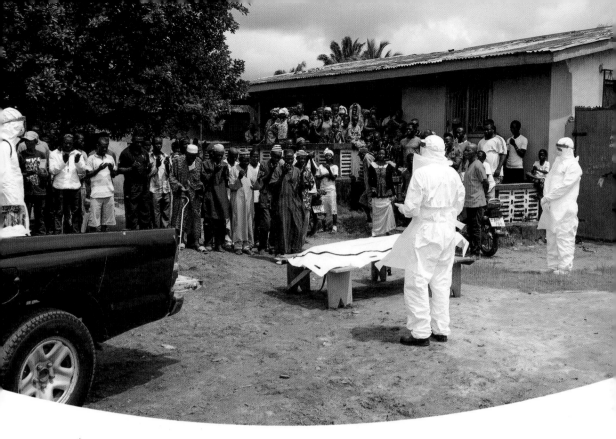

▲ In 2014, Ebola spread in West Africa. Bats carry this disease. Deforestation had forced bats closer to people.

mice and opossums spread less Lyme disease. But places with only mice spread more.

   Certain causes of climate change increase disease as well. For example, deforestation causes animals to lose their homes. Those animals are often forced to move into areas where people live. More contact between people and wild animals increases the chance of a new disease spreading.

CHAPTER 4

CLIMATE SOLUTIONS

In 2018, the United Nations issued a report. It argued that temperatures must not rise more than 2.7 degrees Fahrenheit (1.5°C) above pre-industrial temperatures. Otherwise, people would face catastrophic consequences. The world was already two-thirds of the way to that increased temperature. So, the UN argued for serious action. It said emissions of carbon dioxide should go 45 percent below 2010 levels by 2030.

The United Nations said at least 70 percent of all electricity should come from renewable sources, such as wind power and solar power, by 2050.

By 2050, emissions needed to be at net-zero. Meeting these goals would likely avoid the worst impacts of climate change.

One major solution to climate change is renewable energy. This type of energy uses resources that do not run out. Solar power and wind power are two main kinds. Renewable energy doesn't produce any direct emissions. As a result, it can replace fossil fuels.

With renewable forms of energy, governments can promote electrification. This process means shifting to systems that use electricity. Transportation is an important part of electrification. Instead of gasoline-powered vehicles, people can use electric vehicles. Electric vehicles use powerful batteries to run.

However, electricity use also needs to become more **efficient**. For example, buildings can switch

△ LED light bulbs can be 80 percent more efficient than regular light bulbs.

to LED light bulbs. LEDs use much less energy than regular light bulbs. Cities can improve public transit systems. That way, fewer vehicles could transport the same number of people. As a result, less overall energy would be used.

To meet the UN's goals, industries also need to make large changes. Some involve using different materials. For instance, cement production creates approximately 8 percent of global

CO_2 emissions. So, scientists and engineers are working on lower-carbon ways of making cement.

Agriculture is another key area for reducing emissions. Climate scientists argue that wasting less food will help. Eating more plants and less meat will help, too. Plant-based foods tend to require less energy to produce than meat. Also, farm companies can use greener farming practices, such as using less fertilizer.

In addition, companies and governments can clear fewer forests, especially rainforests. At the same time, people can plant new trees. These actions would take CO_2 out of the atmosphere.

However, these actions will not completely prevent climate change or its negative impacts. For this reason, the UN argued that countries should also focus on adapting to the crisis. For example, coastal areas must adapt to sea level

Coastal wetlands, such as mangroves, can defend against floods and storm surges. They take CO_2 out of the air, too.

rise, floods, and strong storms. Some efforts are human-made, such as seawalls. Other efforts involve developing natural defenses, such as protecting and expanding coastal wetlands.

How much people will have to adapt depends on how well people slow climate change. The more the climate crisis worsens, the more people will have to adapt. The technology and tools to slow climate change already exist. But as of 2022, greenhouse gas emissions were still on the rise.

CHAPTER 5

AVOIDING CLIMATE ACTION

In 2021, only Morocco and The Gambia were on track to keep emissions below the 2.7-degrees-Fahrenheit (1.5°C) goal. India, Costa Rica, Bhutan, Ethiopia, Kenya, and the Philippines were almost there. Most nations were not doing nearly enough. And some countries, including the United States, continued to produce dangerously high emissions.

There were many reasons for this inaction. For one, fossil fuels are key to the world economy.

As of 2022, Morocco had one of the largest solar power plants on Earth.

They provide wealth for industrial nations. Also, fossil fuel companies want to keep their profits. In the 1990s, these companies worked with **conservative** political groups. Together, they spread doubt about climate change.

➤ MEETING CLIMATE TARGETS

This map shows how close countries were in 2021 to reducing greenhouse gas emissions enough to stay below 2.7 degrees Fahrenheit (1.5°C) of warming.

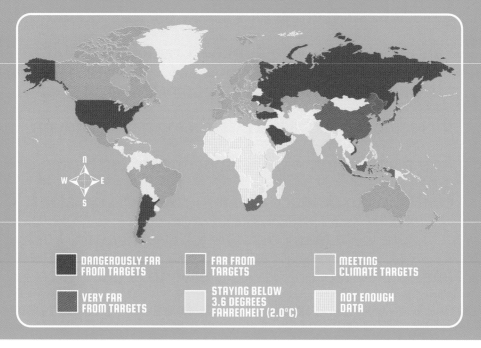

DANGEROUSLY FAR FROM TARGETS

VERY FAR FROM TARGETS

FAR FROM TARGETS

STAYING BELOW 3.6 DEGREES FAHRENHEIT (2.0°C)

MEETING CLIMATE TARGETS

NOT ENOUGH DATA

These efforts succeeded for many years. But by the 2020s, most people believed climate change was happening. Even so, powerful companies and many politicians still tried to prevent action. They used a variety of different arguments to do so.

For instance, some people claimed climate change was a natural process. They said it was caused by the sun. But between the 1980s and 2010s, the sun actually became cooler. Many lawmakers argued climate action was too costly. However, climate experts agreed that the costs of inaction were far greater than the costs of action. In addition, fossil fuel companies worked to place climate responsibility on individuals. But individuals aren't the main cause. A small number of companies produce most global emissions. Plus, individual actions won't be enough to solve the crisis. Only large-scale actions will.

CHAPTER 6

PEOPLE STEP UP

With little climate action from fossil fuel companies and governments, people are stepping up. These actions are taking many forms. For example, climate scientists continue warning people about the crisis. They are also still researching climate change and its effects. In addition, more and more journalists are reporting on the climate crisis. For instance, more weather reporters are linking extreme weather to climate

Research shows that local weather reporters are among the most trusted communicators on climate.

change. These reporters help people understand how the crisis impacts their own lives.

People are developing new climate solutions, too. For instance, some companies have created plant-based foods that taste similar to meat. These companies hope their products will help people eat less meat. That would help reduce greenhouse gas emissions.

Climate **activists** have taken bold actions, too. Some protested the building of new oil pipelines. Others focused on divesting. Divesting involves not giving money to certain companies. Activists encouraged people and groups to divest from fossil fuel companies.

> **THINK ABOUT IT**

Climate change connects to people's lives in many ways. How might education inspire more action?

In September 2019, more than four million youth activists around the world took part in the Global Climate Strike.

Many young people became climate activists. In 2018, Greta Thunberg spoke before the United Nations. She was 15 years old. She told world leaders that young people had a right to live on a planet that had not been destroyed by climate change. She helped lead school strikes around the world. She and many other youth activists skipped school. Instead of going to class, they protested to bring attention to the climate crisis.

Young people also took charge in other ways. For example, Luisa Neubauer of Germany took her country to court. She believed Germany was not doing enough to slow greenhouse gas emissions. Germany's highest court agreed. In 2019, it ruled that the government had to say how it would meet its climate goals. Students around the world have brought similar cases to court.

Indigenous peoples continued their work as land defenders and water protectors. Less than 5 percent of the world's population is Indigenous. Yet Indigenous people manage 80 percent of Earth's biodiversity. The UN argued that Indigenous knowledge can play a key role in working against climate change. To do so, the UN said that Indigenous rights to their lands should

⚠ Nick Tilsen of the Oglala Lakota Nation was one of the leaders who helped stop the Keystone XL oil pipeline.

be respected. They have tended to these regions for thousands of years.

People's climate action and activism helped make the crisis a higher priority in politics. Lawmakers began to listen. In 2021, US lawmakers started pushing harder than ever for serious climate action.

ALEXANDRIA VILLASEÑOR

In November 2018, 13-year-old Alexandria Villaseñor smelled smoke. The Camp Fire was raging in Northern California. The wildfire was among the deadliest in California history. It destroyed 15,000 homes and killed 86 people. The Camp Fire was miles away from Alexandria. But the smoke still reached her. Plus, Alexandria had asthma. As a result, the smoke made it hard for her to breathe. She went home to New York to stay safe. Even then, she still had to go to the emergency room to control her asthma attack.

Alexandria decided to learn more about wildfires and climate change. She learned how the climate crisis was already impacting her. Within a month, she joined Greta Thunberg outside the United Nations. They protested government

Alexandria Villaseñor (center) went to a climate event with activists Xiye Bastida (left) and Greta Thunberg in 2019.

inaction on climate change. She kept protesting every Friday outside the UN for more than a year.

In 2019, Alexandria continued her climate work. She joined 15 other young activists in filing a complaint to the UN. They wanted to force governments to act on climate change. Alexandria also started Earth Uprising. This group educates young people on the crisis. It also helps organize youth who want to become climate activists.

CHAPTER 7

LOOKING AHEAD

As of 2022, the climate crisis was still getting worse. Earth's temperature was rising faster. As a result, other changes were also accelerating. Scientists believed the changes in climate were close to hitting dangerous tipping points. A tipping point is a small shift that leads to a sudden, massive change. These massive changes could last for hundreds of years. For example, rising temperatures could melt the Arctic

From 1992 to 2001, Greenland lost 34 billion tons (31 billion metric tons) of ice per year. From 2002 to 2020, it lost eight times that amount.

permafrost. The permafrost is a layer of Earth that is always frozen. If it melted, the soil would release vast amounts of methane into the air. The sudden increase in greenhouse gases would rapidly increase Earth's temperature. As a result, much more climate change would quickly take place. That new change could then trigger a new tipping point and even larger negative impacts.

Climate scientists and activists warned others about these effects. Some even said such changes could cause entire societies to collapse. However, scientists stressed that there was always time for change. Every bit of reduced emissions can help.

➢ THINK ABOUT IT

What adults could you talk to about climate change?
What specific information would you share with them?

y

Research shows that adults are often most influenced by their children in conversations about climate change.

Young people often led these calls for change. Around the world, they organized and worked together. Many young people began by talking with their families. They discussed with their parents why climate change mattered to them. These conversations helped spread concern about the crisis. Once enough people organized together for change, serious solutions could become reality.

FOCUS ON
THE CLIMATE CRISIS

Write your answers on a separate piece of paper.

1. Write a letter to an adult describing what you learned about adapting to the climate crisis.

2. Are you interested in taking action to help slow climate change? Why or why not? If you are, what actions could you take?

3. Between the 1750s and 2010s, the United States was responsible for what percentage of all CO_2 emissions?

    A. less than 6 percent
    B. approximately 15 percent
    C. approximately 25 percent

4. Why does the climate crisis affect wealthy countries less than low-income countries?

    A. Wealthy countries have done more to prevent the climate crisis.
    B. Wealthy countries have more resources to adapt to the climate crisis.
    C. Climate change affects only the areas where low-income countries are.

Answer key on page 48.

GLOSSARY

acidic
Having a chemical property that can break some things down.

activists
People who take action to make social or political changes.

biodiversity
The number of different species that live in an area.

climate change
A human-caused global crisis involving long-term changes in Earth's temperature and weather patterns.

conservative
Supporting traditional views or values, often resisting changes.

efficient
Accomplishing as much as possible with as little effort or as few resources as possible.

Indigenous
Native to a region, or belonging to ancestors who lived in a region before colonists arrived.

Industrial Revolution
Starting in Great Britain in the 1700s, a huge economic shift involving the use of powerful machines and mass production.

pathogens
Viruses, bacteria, or parasites that can spread disease.

photosynthesis
The process in which plants turn sunlight, carbon dioxide, and water into oxygen and energy.

TO LEARN MORE

BOOKS

Kallen, Stuart A. *Extreme Weather and Climate Change: What's the Connection?* San Diego: ReferencePoint Press, 2022.

McPherson, Stephanie Sammartino. *Hothouse Earth: The Climate Crisis and the Importance of Carbon Neutrality.* Minneapolis: Lerner Publications, 2021.

Stratton, Connor. *Bias in Reporting on Climate Change.* Lake Elmo, MN: Focus Readers, 2021.

NOTE TO EDUCATORS

Visit **www.focusreaders.com** to find lesson plans, activities, links, and other resources related to this title.

INDEX

Answer Key: 1. Answers will vary; **2.** Answers will vary; **3.** C; **4.** B